Stephen A. Surace is a consulta
speaker. After a rapid rise up tl   ̶ ̶ ̶ ̶ ̶ ̶ ̶ ̶ ̶ ̶ ̶ at a relatively
young age, Stephen decided to help others in their pursuits of
success. He studied Computer Engineering at the University
of Connecticut, and currently resides in Connecticut with his
wife and dog.

For contact details and other information, please visit:
StephenASurace.com.

CONFIDENCE

The Formula for Resume and Interview Success

STEPHEN A. SURACE

To Roz
With (lots of)
Love!

Steph Su

ISBN 978-1-7329409-0-1

Cover design by Allison Nottingham

Contents

Introduction   1

1: Burning Bridges   3

2: The Resume   5

3: Resume FAQs   15

4: Interviews Overview   19

5: What Are They Looking For   21

6: Your Example Stories   22

7: Two Common Questions   27

8: Interview FAQs   32

Conclusion   40

To my mother and father, who, together,
always instilled in me great confidence.

Introduction

Landing the right job means more than just making more money or having a sexier title. At times, it can mean better relationships at home, an improved work-life balance, and even greater health. We spend a lot of time at work—about 1,800 hours a year on average in the U.S.—so why not spend that time in an environment you enjoy, while doing work you find fulfilling?

Within this book, I have laid out my best techniques for helping others land their next job advancements, and thus, life upgrades. The tips I describe come from years of assisting countless individuals with resume and interview preparation. In hiring for my own teams, I have gone through numerous resumes, and conducted hundreds of interviews. I know what catches my eyes and those of my fellow executives.

When interviewing candidates, I often find most are unprepared in truly describing the value they bring. Many candidates appear nervous and may only crack a smile once the whole encounter is over. My goal in writing this book is to bring awareness, confidence, and a simple plan for success as you look to advance your career. Whether you are currently job searching or not, you will be well prepared when the time comes for the next opportunity.

Getting that amazing job is possible. Speaking positively about yourself without sounding like a braggart most definitely is achievable. Follow the actions suggested in this book and you will be comfortable and confident in documenting your wins and in presenting yourself to a room full of strangers.

I kept this book brief on purpose. Often times, we do not have time to finish a large book before an interview. This is meant to be a quick guide—one that can be referenced repeatedly, or even used to prepare for your interview tomorrow.

I start the book with a word of caution, followed by tips on structuring your resume to get noticed. Finally, I go into detail on how to best prepare for any interview. Naturally, most of the book is focused on interviews. That is where the bulk of time is spent in the hiring process, and, therefore, a majority of the preparation is required.

I am always open to feedback, and hope to hear of the great successes my readers have after applying these concepts.

Let's get to it.

1: Burning Bridges

Be careful! The contents of this book may make you extremely confident in being able to obtain your next amazing job. That is great! However, this newfound confidence should not become a distraction at your current job. When an employee knows they have a new job in hand it can lead them to act differently at work before they move on. So, a warning: do NOT burn bridges.

Perhaps your company is heading toward bankruptcy, or layoffs are imminent. Maybe the culture has changed to the point where internal actions no longer mirror what its founders intended the company to stand for. Perhaps there really is no other upward movement for you there. What do you do?

If you know in your heart you ultimately want to leave your current employer, be sure to maintain good relationships with your coworkers. You never know when you will see them again. In a strange twist of fate, maybe they become your boss one day.

If you give your two-week notice, then during those two weeks, you should perform at the same high level as before. Do not slack off, or say, "It's your problem now; I'm gone in T-minus two days!" Do not show up an hour late or leave an hour early. Your coworkers are watching, and their good impression of you can change instantly with that kind of negative behavior.

If you are leaving, give your coworkers enough notice to prepare for a smooth departure. Ensure others can handle your work in your absence, and that all knowledge transfer is complete before your last day. Try to get in touch with everyone who relies on you or has invested time in you to let them know personally that you will be moving on. They will appreciate finding out from you rather than three weeks later when an email to you bounces back with an error.

Others may ask why you are leaving. When voicing reasons for your departure, there is no need to vilify the company or others. Keep things positive. Use phrases such as:

- "I found a great opportunity elsewhere."
- "This new job is more in line with my long-term goals."
- "The position better suits the needs of my family."

How you exit a company speaks volumes about who you are. Maintaining relationships with your network is important. If you treat them well, they will be there for life. You never know if they may help connect you with a job in the future.

2: The Resume

Your resume is the tool that helps get you noticed. Whether you are applying to a job directly, or being referred from a friend, your resume is required. The secret to a great resume is demonstrating your value effectively. Here is how you begin doing that.

ACTION 1: Document your wins every week (with metrics).

Even if you are not in the midst of a job search, I always recommend documenting your "wins" every week. A win is any positive outcome of which you were a part. Wins come in all sizes: small, large, and everything in between. At first, the act of reflecting on your workweek and keeping a tally of wins may seem a bit foreign. After a few weeks, however, you may go from struggling to identify one or two items, to listing five or six consistently. This weekly 5-minute exercise helps to put the rest of your work into perspective. You may find that this exercise results in an almost subconscious nudge toward taking more positive action with your future work activities.

A quick side note for those in leadership roles: If you are a people manager, the achievements of your employees are also considered your accomplishments. If your team completes a successful project under your guidance, for example, that is also your win.

A critical component to any win is its measurement. This is a metric which helps to demonstrate the positive change. Everything can have a measurement associated with it: time, money, morale, sales, customer satisfaction, attrition, speed, quality, security, productivity, engagement, risk, compliance, and so forth.

Each of your wins should have a related measurement. In most cases, this means understanding what the baseline was before your positive change was implemented. For example, if you are leading a project to simplify order processing, take a measurement of what the current order processing times are. Let's say an order currently takes six days for processing. After several weeks, you help to institute multiple changes, which result in a 50% reduction in processing times. Now, orders only take three days to process. This is great! Others will better appreciate the value you brought to order processing knowing both the baseline and end result.

Wins do not always have to be the result of large projects. The new employee you helped gave your manager positive feedback about you after her first week. That is a win, and the measurement for which could be ramp-up time. How fast did the previous employee get up to speed without your help compared to the new employee you assisted? What about the course you took proactively to sharpen your skills, which resulted in you being more efficient? That is a win. Or the meeting you called to get feedback on an idea, which resulted in an even better concept being formulated by the group. That is a win. It may seem like just setting up a meeting to you, but the result had a positive impact. What if you did not set up that meeting? What if you were not open-minded toward others' opinions? What if you did not have the right people in the room? Would the new idea have been conceived otherwise?

Do not dismiss wins simply because they may appear trivial to you. This could cause you to miss the bigger picture of the true value you bring. The exercise of continuously documenting wins will help you see how you are positively impacting yourself, your team, your customers, and your company.

Your weekly list of wins will grow, and can be used to highlight your achievements for any time period: the month, the quarter, the year, etc. It especially may be useful for performance review discussions or annual self-assessments. Of course, many of the best wins throughout the year will make it onto your resume.

ACTION 2: Add your best and most relevant wins under each job in your resume.

So, you have your key wins from your current and previous jobs. Now, choose the most impactful and add them as brief bullets in your resume under each job. Pick the most relevant examples that best demonstrate your capabilities and value to a company.

Each job you apply for will likely require tweaks in your resume to ensure relevancy. You want to make sure the skills required for the job are reflected in your resume. For example, let's say you are in advertising sales and are applying for a role managing accounts of consumer packaged goods (CPG) clients. While you could highlight your experience working with healthcare and pharmaceutical clients, it would be best to make your prior experience with CPG brands more prominent. Those CPG-related bullets would move to the top of your lists, and non-CPG items could move down or be removed altogether.

Furthermore, your value should be quantifiable. This is where the metrics described in Action 1 come into play. Writing something like, "I helped save the company money," does not show your value as well as, "Reduced cost of running the XYZ process by $35,000 per year."

Write your wins as short bullets, so that anyone reading your resume can understand them. This means avoiding internal acronyms or system names, which only your coworkers would know. If you worked on the "Porsche System," which was the code name for the internal auditing tool, then just call it the "internal auditing system." If you actually worked on a Porsche, then by all means put that down.

Ensure that each bullet starts with a verb. If it is something you did in the past, put it in the past tense. If it is something you are currently doing, make it present tense. Here are some examples of past-tense action words (and their present-tense counterparts) with which to start your sentences:

- Achieved (Achieving)
- Executed (Executing)
- Led (Leading)
- Created (Creating)
- Enhanced (Enhancing)
- Managed (Managing)
- Designed (Designing)
- Decreased (Decreasing)
- Increased (Increasing)
- Advised (Advising)
- Partnered (Partnering)
- Eliminated (Eliminating)

When drafting your resume, please do not list out your job description in each role. When I review resumes, I find this practice to be quite bothersome. I am not looking for what your previous employers *expected* of you. I am trying to learn what you *actually* delivered or accomplished. Each and every bullet should be a key win with an associated metric to help demonstrate value. If you feel strongly that a brief one-liner is required to explain the role a bit, put that first above your "wins" list. Even that one-liner should contain metrics, if possible (things like how many employees you led, size of budget you managed, etc.).

Let's look at a few examples that explain what I mean.

Nick was a financial analyst. He had a way with spreadsheets, formulas, and calculations. At the end of each quarter, Nick and his teammates had to crunch the numbers to help close the books. The process took about 12 business days.

Everyone in the office knew not to bother Nick and his team during quarter-end. If the books were not closed on time, the company could face financial penalties. As a result, no one on the team was allowed to take time off during the last two weeks of each quarter. It was not uncommon for people to put in 12-hour days or be required to come in over the weekend. It was grueling.

Nick, however, noticed several inefficiencies within the process. The week after the quarter ended, he jotted some notes down on where he experienced the most "pain" throughout the process. Here are just a few of those:

- Physically scanning over 200 documents one-by-one and hand-delivering them to accounting in the building across the street.
- Waiting for the total asset numbers to load into the system nightly; any revision then required another 24 hours to be reflected in the system.
- Manual calculations from the team in South America caused many iterations and last-minute changes to the numbers.

Nick collected his notes and requested time to review them with his manager. His manager appreciated the insight. So,

Nick asked if he could set up a meeting to have others provide their feedback and opinions on what they would like to see improved.

Nick's meeting with the team went well, and it sparked many ideas. He took the lead on managing the implementation of the changes. Some of those changes were in place by the next quarter, while others took longer, as they required larger technical system enhancements in partnership with IT.

After one year, Nick's improvements helped the team cut out seven days of the overall process. And on top of that, the remaining five days were "normal" workdays, and no one had to stay late or work over the weekend. That is a quantifiable impact—and a major one at that!

So, how did Nick list this on his resume? Here's his bullet:

- Led improvement efforts for financial quarter-end processes, resulting in 58% reduction in time (12 days to 5 days) to complete each cycle.

Notice how it starts with an action verb ("led") and is in the past tense because it is something that he has accomplished already. In addition, he put the percentage reduction in terms anyone can understand: 12 days to 5 days.

You may ask, "But Nick did so much—why such a short bullet on that great accomplishment?"

There are a few reasons for this:

1. Nick has other bullets to add under this Financial Analyst role—this is not his only win to highlight.
2. We want to keep the resume brief and to the point. Often times, hiring managers or recruiting personnel are overloaded with resumes for a job opening. This means it is unlikely they will be spending a lot of time on each one. Remember, the goal is to demonstrate quantifiable results and value quickly.

3. When Nick is asked to come in for an interview, he will
    have plenty of time to describe what he did in more
    detail. More on that in the following chapters.

Let's look at another example of how wins on the job can
translate to quantifiable highlights on the resume.

Jen specialized in marketing at an advertising agency. Her
group was tasked with launching an ad campaign for a regional
chain of grocery stores looking to grow their home delivery
service.

Jen devised an online advertising strategy across social media
and traditional media websites. Her goal was to attract shoppers
in the region to the grocer's online delivery services.

Before the campaign launched, Jen took a baseline of visits
and sales of the delivery service website. Immediately after
starting her campaign, it became apparent her advertising
strategy was working. Visits to the site tripled, and home
delivery sales were up 58%. In addition, customers who clicked
on the ads spent 17% more ($68 vs. $58) than those who visited
the site organically.

Here is what Jen put on her resume for this accomplishment:

- Implemented ad campaign for Acme Grocery; drove
  58% increase in home delivery sales and 17% increase i
  average online spend per customer ($68 vs. $58).

There are many ways Jen could have crafted her bullet
above. If she had sales numbers in dollar amounts, those could
have been included. If the grocer made significantly more in
profit than the cost of the ad campaign, that could have been
highlighted. In addition, if the grocery chain came back for
repeat business, that is another win. When there are numerous

large wins under one topic, it is possible to list them as separate sub-bullets.

Be aware of the sensitivity of certain metrics: specific sales numbers, profit margins, or engagement costs may be considered confidential and may not be appropriate for a resume.

ACTION 3: Create your profile.

The very first section of the resume after your contact info should be your profile. The profile section is 2-3 sentences describing yourself in a way which summarizes your key work experiences, passions, and expertise.

I recommend titling this section the exact job title of the role you are applying for. I recommend this for two reasons: first, it helps you remember which resume version you used to apply; and second, it helps your resume get a boost by any algorithms sorting through hundreds of applications. (Note: the more key words from the job description that also appear in your resume, the better. For example, if the role requires skills in software development, but you have been using the term "software engineering" in your resume, change it to match their terminology.)

The content of the profile section is important because sometimes it may be the only thing recruiters glance at. It could be your one chance to get noticed in a sea of resumes.

In order to really stand out, you need to know what your audience is looking for. Do your research on the role and tailor your profile toward the experience and passions you have which will help the company succeed.

This is not the place for clichés or ambiguous adjectives. Avoid using terms like: hard-working, team player, results-oriented, etc. Those are great, but they are subjective. What exactly does results-oriented mean? Focus instead on more

objective things: years of experience, major responsibilities, accomplishments, passions, certifications, etc.
Here are some example profiles:

Counselor:
Experienced school counselor passionate about the comprehensive development of students. Proficiency at the middle and high-school levels. Well-versed at building positive rapport with diverse student populations.

Software Developer:
Senior software developer with over 12 years of hands-on software development experience across web and mobile applications. Skilled in building secure and scalable applications serving millions of global users. Two apps ranked in Apple's top 100 list in 2017.

Customer Service:
Customer service specialist with over 3 years experience in building strong relationships between customers and brands. Developed strategies for improving customer satisfaction by 32%. Recognized as highest-rated service agent by customer surveys.

Healthcare:
Certified Family Nurse Practitioner passionate about women's health with 8 years of experience caring for underserved populations. Successfully partner with local government organizations to drive health education and positive outcomes.

Marketing:
Marketing director with 18 years of experience building consumer brands and driving sales. Passionate about cultivating

customer-focused teams and a positive work culture. Recognized by *Ad Week* as one of top 50 most influential marketers in 2018.

Sales:
Senior sales leader experienced in healthcare and pharmaceutical verticals, responsible for over $35 million in annual revenue. Passionate about mentoring and building high-performing sales teams. Named to "Chairman's Circle" past 3 years for being in top 1% of all sales reps nationwide.

Product Owner:
Certified Scrum Product Owner (CSPO) experienced in leading the development of financial software in support of Sales and Marketing. Deep working knowledge of Agile practices and test-driven development. Well-versed in translating key business objectives and financial regulations to technical team.

3: Resume FAQs

What about the objective section?

I hope by now you can see the point of the resume is to demonstrate the value you bring *to* a company or organization. The traditional objective statement describes what you want from an organization. Therefore, I recommend the objective statement be left out of any resume. We all know your objective anyway: to land the job!

How should I arrange the order of my resume?

Most items in the resume are listed in chronological order, with the most recent on top. This means your current job should be first under the work experience section, followed by your previous role, and so on. The same applies for the education section: your most recent degree information is listed first.

Remember, when it comes to the individual bullets underneath your jobs, the items most impactful and most relevant to the role are listed first.

Where does my education section go? Should I include my graduation year?

If you are still in school, it goes toward the top (with expected graduation date). If you have ever worked anywhere post schooling, it goes at the bottom (with the graduation year optional—I prefer leaving it out).

What about my role in that company 22 years ago?

Employers will be looking at your resume with a mentality of, "What have you done for me lately?" Only keep to the most relevant experience on your resume. Your list of wins under each role should be the largest under your most recent roles. No need to go into that much detail on roles held 20-plus years ago. In fact, those roles may not even be worth mentioning. Use your judgment. If you are going into three pages due to your lengthy work history, cut it off and stick to two pages.

What if I had a gap in employment?

You may have taken time off to raise a newborn, help with an elderly parent, or just had a hard time getting a new job after a layoff. Here are a few things you can do:

1. Explain the gap. You can list what you did during that time, but also what you did to keep your skills sharp Perhaps you took a few online courses, attended workshops, obtained a new certification, joined a local non-profit, or volunteered your services. This shows that you proactively looked to remain current in your skills.

2. Never lie. If it took you 18 months to land a new job after a layoff, for example, you can list the dates of employment as years instead of months and years. For example, if you worked at Company A from March 2009 to February 2014, you can put 2009-2014. If you did not get a job again until August 2015 at Company B, you can list Company B's dates as 2015-2018. As long as you are consistent in using the same format for all roles, that is fine. Just be prepared to discuss specifics at the

interview, including examples of things you did to keep
your skills sharp.

What about an executive summary or key accomplishments section?

If you held a lot of roles and feel the need to summarize the
most relevant and impactful wins at the top, you can do that.
That section can go immediately after your profile. The list
of accomplishments should not be more than five or six and
should all have metrics associated with them demonstrating the
value you helped deliver.

Do you have examples of resume templates or outlines?

Yes. To download a sample resume outline, visit my website:
StephenASurace.com.

Do these resume tips apply to medical doctors?

Likely not. A small amount of professions have very
different resume standards. Physician resumes are one of those.
I do have a sample physician resume template on my website:
StephenASurace.com.

I can play five different instruments—where do I list that?

Extra-curricular activities are fantastic, but may not always
be relevant to the role. If you are applying to be a music teacher,
for example, it definitely is relevant in this case. But if you are
applying for an accounting role, it likely is not and can be left
out.

My resume is just over one page. What should I do?

I recommend sticking to one page when possible. You can do two pages if you have a significant amount of accomplishments, but only if it reaches the halfway point of the second page or beyond. You do not want one full page and just a few lines on page two.

To make everything fit, consider reducing the size of the font and margins. I do not recommend using a font size smaller than 10. Also, be sure the margins are not so small that the text gets cut off when the resume is printed.

Do you have any other tips?

Be consistent. If you put a period at the end of one bullet point, be sure to put one at the end of each one. Spacing, punctuation, and font size should all be consistent throughout the resume. This both keeps it readable and shows your attention to detail.

4: Interviews Overview

I was trained by a Fortune 10 company in interviewer skills. This was not just any interviewer training—this was intense. Numerous hours of lectures, followed by practice sessions, workshops, and tests. All of this culminated in real interviews where we assessed candidates, while simultaneously being assessed by our instructors. The course was incredible.

After conducting countless interviews with this process, I began receiving requests for interview help from job seekers. So, like any engineer might do, I decided to reverse-engineer the interviewer process I learned. My goal was to take this great tool I had for discovering top talent, and, in essence, rearrange it in a way that enables individuals to better describe themselves. I needed to make it generic enough to fit any company and any profession. And that is exactly what I did.

The following sections describe my "engineered" process for preparing for interviews. My approach is to prepare you so well that the interview feels like a pleasant conversation about yourself, and not something you are nervous about. You will find that the preparation is where the hard work happens; the interview is where you shine. My goal is to enable you to articulate the best values of yourself the first time, and leave feeling you put your best foot forward.

These techniques have proven to work across all industries and job types: technology, education, law, retail, finance, and many in between. The tips below are most useful during the first few rounds of interviews. This is normally where the behavioral-based questions are asked. Behavioral-based questions are generally focused on how you act at work—the way you handle situations, people, or tasks. These tend to be questions like: "Tell me about a time when you had to present a new idea to management—how did you do it?"; "Describe a time you had to deal with a difficult customer—how did you handle it?"

Ultimately, you need to possess the specific skills of the job you are applying for. If you are applying for a very technical role, like mechanical engineer, these techniques will most certainly help you, but you will still need to know the laws of thermodynamics, for example. That, I am afraid, is something I cannot help you with. My three-step action plan helps you better demonstrate the skills and traits that you currently possess.

5: What Are They Looking For?

The first step of my process is to understand what type of candidate the role requires.

ACTION 1: List the top 10 traits you think the job requires an individual to possess.

This must be done from the employer's perspective. In other words, think about it as if you were already working at that company—what would you look for in candidates? To do this, I first suggest looking for clues in the job description. Are there any adjectives that jump out or are used often? What are some traits required to solve some of the challenges listed in the job responsibilities? Next, go to the company's website or marketing material. What types of values does the company tout? Are there any trends in the language they use in describing themselves, their people, or their results? Try to identify what you believe are 10 key traits the job requires.

Each company is different, but here are some examples that I have seen: integrity, great communication, team player, innovative, strong leader, etc.

6: Your Example Stories

The second step is to demonstrate to the employer that you possess the key traits they are looking for.

ACTION 2: For each key trait you identified in Action 1, think of two work-related examples of you demonstrating that trait.

Each example, or short story, should focus on you and have a positive outcome or learning. You should have 15 to 20 stories in total. I call them "stories" because they have a distinct beginning, middle, and end. This outline is deliberate, as it ensures you never fumble when providing answers to interview questions. These types of stories will help you answer just about any behavioral-based interview question you are asked. In fact, I tell folks if they do this well, they definitely will get past the first interview and be invited for the next round. So far, I have been right.

Here is the story format I recommend:

1. *Beginning: A brief overview of the problem, challenge, or task.*
    The overview helps set the stage for your response. It ensures everyone understands what you are talking about. Since your stories are related to traits the company is looking for, these will likely resonate with your interviewers. You have their attention.

2. *Middle: What you did to solve, overcome, or complete it.*
    Now that you have captured their attention, outline
    the steps you took to solve the challenge or complete
    the task at hand. I stress the word "you" because too
    often folks will focus on "we" and "the team" here. Yes,
    it is great that you are a team player, but what
    specifically did you do that was great? They are not
    looking to hire your team; they are looking to hire you.

3. *End: The positive outcome or results.*
    The key to ending a story is to articulate the positive
    effect you made. This ensures that each of your
    responses ends on a positive note and demonstrates
    your value. Usually, it is best when the value can be
    described in terms of a measurement (i.e., can be
    quantified), since people can put it into better
    perspective.

Jeremy, a friend of mine, came to me after going on five
different interviews at five different companies. He did not
receive a single call back from any of them. He felt frustrated
and dejected. From my perspective, he had all the necessary
skills and experience needed to be successful at all five of those
companies. I thought to myself, his resume is written well
since it got him in the door of five employers, so there must be
something wrong with how he is handling interviews.

I suggested he spend some time with me before his next
interview to learn the method of preparing example stories. He
agreed. About a week before his next interview, we sat down
to outline the key traits we believed the company was looking
for. He was able to list out nine. From there, I asked him for two
work-related examples to help demonstrate how he possesses
each of those traits. I assisted him in formulating his examples
into the proper structure: overview of the problem or challenge,

what he did to solve it, and the positive outcome. We finished with six stories, and he completed another ten over the next few days on his own.

Jeremy went into the interview with those 16 example stories ready in his mind. And he nailed it. He ended up getting called back for another round of interviews and, ultimately, landed the role. He said the stories gave him confidence knowing that the responses he presented were the most impactful, demonstrating his true worth.

(Side note: If you look closely at the last three paragraphs above, you will see the same format being used: overview of the problem, what I did to solve it, and the positive result.)

Let's take a look at some examples of well-structured example stories.

Anthony was a lab manager at a biotech firm selling special gels for scientific research. The trait he wanted to exemplify with this story is "problem solving." Here is his story:

> We had been getting calls from angry customers about a new product we just started shipping. We guarantee 99.99% success, but about 30% of the new product we shipped seemed to be failing.
>
> I immediately called a meeting with the quality control team, and put a plan together to try to replicate the failures our customers experienced. We were able to replicate the issue. So, I worked to identify a solution, and found a relatively inexpensive fix with a particular solvent. If I coated each gel with this solvent, it did not fail when it was put through testing. I proposed to management that we test this solution further, and if it works, we coat all the products with this mixture before shipping to customers.
>
> The solution worked. The company did not have to scrap thousands of unused products, and all shipments of the new

product had 100% success rate thereafter.

Anthony's story was short and to the point (as it should be), and it followed the same structure: a brief background on the problem, steps he took to solve it, and the positive, measurable results.

Anthony did not memorize his stories word for word, but rather remembered the basic outline and the examples he wanted to talk about. The one above was the product launch failure story. He could recite it any time because he lived through the issue at work firsthand. He went through the emotions of managing angry customer calls and realizing a new product potentially may need to be scrapped. He remembers the pressure he felt of needing to find a solution, and the late hours he put in during his testing. In the end, Anthony remained calm and his quick-thinking saved the company a lot of money. That is a great example of problem solving.

But is it also a great example of dealing with difficult customers? Or communicating new ideas with management? Or showing creativity? Or demonstrating influence?

Yes. Yes. And yes.

That is the beauty of preparing your example stories. They usually can apply to numerous different traits, which means they can be used to answer many different questions asked during the interview.

This also is why one should never be overly concerned about the exact question they may be asked or the exact trait the interviewer may be looking for. There is no need to think, "Are they asking about communication or creativity here?" Often times, it is not just one trait, while other times, it may not be any particular trait at all. In the end, if your interviewer needs further clarification, they will ask.

Lastly, your example stories are meant to be brief and to the point. The more succinct they are, the more stories you will be able to present. This is good, because all your stories paint you in a positive light. If you only are able to present two or three stories in a single interview you are doing yourself a disservice by getting too granular in the details. Keep your stories high level and stick to the outline: What was the challenge? (1-3 sentences.) What did you do to solve it? (1-4 sentences.) What was the positive outcome? (1-3 sentences.)

7: Two Common Questions

Sometimes, I am asked which questions to prepare for before an interview. One can find hundreds of common interview questions online, but odds are you will not be asked those. Every company is different, and every interviewer is different. I tell people to spend their time honing their example stories, and not to drown in the very low-odds game of interview question roulette. However, there are two questions that I always prepare folks for. In thinking of answers for these two questions, candidates learn to see themselves in a more positive way, which helps them better articulate their value.

ACTION 3: Prepare for these two common questions: "Can you tell me a little about yourself" and "Why should we hire you?"

Question 1: "Can you tell me a little about yourself?"

This question usually is asked first. It is a nice "settling-in" question. The interviewer feels like they are throwing out a warm-up pitch, and the interviewee gets excited because they know they can nail this one. Everyone wins! Right?

Not quite.

Many candidates drop the ball on this prime opportunity to make a stellar first impression. The most common answer I get to this question is a regurgitation of the candidate's resume. If I wanted someone to recite the resume, I would have asked, "Can you please verbally list out everything which I already know about you?" The positive first impression opportunity is lost at that point.

The best answers I have received to my asking, "Tell me about yourself," have been given by candidates, who describe themselves in ways that cannot be gleaned directly from their resume. They use it to describe passions, and, therefore, they speak with an energy and contagious enthusiasm. This question, I argue, is not a warm-up question; it very well could be the question which helps land you the job.

When preparing an answer for, "Tell me about yourself," do not think of all the jobs you had or degrees you earned. Think about what you are most excited about doing as a result of your experience and skills, and relate that to your beliefs, ideals and how you see yourself as a person. Do this correctly and you may find yourself speaking with such passion that you surprise even yourself.

Allow me to give a couple of examples. Let's start with Alex:

Alex was a soccer coach. She had been coaching youth teams for over eight years at the highest skill levels, and won numerous awards and championships. She was applying for a varsity head coach position at a local high school when she reached out to me for help. Before her interview, I suggested she polish her "tell me about yourself" response. She did, and, like clockwork, she got that question immediately after walking into the room of interviewers.

Alex responded by speaking about her love of coaching, and how she believes it positively impacts youths' lives. She spoke about the joy she gets watching her players grow from adolescents to young adults through not just her soccer coaching, but also her mentorship.

Alex's answer was genuine and heartfelt, and made a big impact on the interviewers. Alex won them over from the beginning. There was no mention of past championships or trophies won (besides, those were already listed on the resume). Alex focused on the things that meant the most to her with regard to the position she was applying. Her response was about her, but worded in a way that highlights the more profound human-level connections of how she views her work. It painted Alex in a positive light, one that was not immediately clear from her resume.

That is the beauty of this question. It allows you to answer in a way where others with the same passion feel an instant connection to you. They are connected to your emotions, your principles, and the positive energy and enthusiasm that shine through your response.

How do *you* think you would answer this question if asked? Many people find their answer is easier to formulate when the question is restated as: "What excites you most about your work?"; "What about this role motivates you?"; or "Where do you find your passion at work?"

Here is another example:

Audrey was a senior recruiter. She helped source individuals for open positions at the companies that contracted her. She had a great talent in matching individuals to roles in which they can thrive.

Audrey was up against another candidate for a promotion within her company, and was asked to interview with senior management as part of the process. Audrey was a bit nervous, mostly because the company just hired a new chief operating officer, and she knew he would be leading the interview. Audrey wished the previous COO had not left because she had such a great rapport with her. I encouraged Audrey to prepare for the "Tell me about yourself" question. Sure enough, she was asked by the COO, "Can you tell me a little about yourself?" Here is what she said:

I am passionate about helping others. Being a recruiter means I can do that every day by helping to place people in jobs where they can succeed and enjoy going to work. I love making connections with my clients and candidates, and keep in touch with many of them years after I helped to get them placed. I take great pride in knowing I have a positive impact on people's lives.

Audrey described her passions. She spoke about what excites her at work, and how it impacts her personally. The new COO was very impressed. Of course, Audrey also was well prepared for the numerous other questions, but I believe this particular answer helped gain the immediate attention of the COO.

Audrey got the promotion. She was named vice president and put in charge of managing a team of 12 recruiters.

As you can see, "Tell me about yourself" is not a warm-up pitch. This is not a time to repeat what they already know. This is where you can immediately shine and connect with the people in the room.

Question 2: "Why should we hire you?"

This question may not come up as often, but I like to prepare candidates for this because it forces them to think about the value they can bring to an organization. You would be surprised how many people cannot answer this question without fumbling during my interview prep sessions. After identifying the list of traits and preparing 15-20 example stories, some people still cannot seem to summarize their value concisely. So, I hear responses like this:

Me: "Danny, why should we hire you?"

Danny: "Uh, because, I, uh..."

I suggest answering this question by identifying the key themes and greatest impact you made in your example stories. The strengths, accomplishments, and experience you have which best match the role will be what you highlight in your answer. Think about the outcomes you create, and the value you have brought to your team and company. If you look at your example stories, you should find 2-3 themes arise, which summarize your value. Also, your "Tell me about yourself" response usually has some strengths hidden in there as well.

Of course, there is no right or wrong answer here, but I do recommend ensuring the answer you provide is aligned with the role and the traits you wrote down in Action 1.

Take Jon as an example. Jon is a software engineer. He applied for a role at a financial firm requiring skills in some of his favorite computer programming languages. The job required collaborating with coworkers in Marketing, Sales, and IT to build and enhance their internal software systems.

Jon believed the top traits from Action 1 for this role were: proactive, collaborative, technical competence, and eagerness to learn. So his answer to the "Why should we hire you?" question went something like this:

I believe my understanding of U.S. banking regulations and deep expertise in software make me a great fit for this role. In my current role at ACME National Bank, I built systems that support over 15 million users with 150 million transactions each month. The latest project I completed in collaboration with IT and Marketing enabled customers to deposit checks using their mobile phone. The image recognition technology used was something I learned on my own outside of work and brought in as a prototype. I believe this experience and my eagerness to learn can help ABC Bank elevate its digital products.

8: Interview FAQs

What if I finish giving my example story in response to a question, but the interviewer does not say anything?

This can be an awkward situation. The candidate answers the question fully, and then pauses to allow the interviewer to either respond or move to the next question. However, the interviewer does not say anything, and a few seconds manage to feel like an eternity. As a result, the candidate feels the need to fill "dead air."

This is where things could go south quickly. The candidate may resort to saying things that they did not prepare just because they think they have to continue to speak.

For this scenario, I always advise candidates to pause and wait a bit for the interviewer to collect their thoughts. Be comfortable with the silence. If you feel the need to break the silence, I suggest to simply ask, "Did that answer your question?"

What if I don't have a positive result for an example story?

Sometimes, your hard work might not result in the outcome you hoped for. Perhaps you persevered through many obstacles to launch a new product, advertising campaign, or internal process, only to find it did not succeed in one form or another. In cases like this, I am certain if you look beyond the immediate perceived failure there is some learning—some nuggets of wisdom—that came out of it.

Learning is a positive result. If your example story ended with a failed product, for example, state what you learned from that experience. Or perhaps explain what you would have done differently next time. Or describe how your next product launch was a success because of what you learned. The wisdom you gain from challenging experiences is valuable.

What if they ask me one of those strange questions like, "If you could be an animal, which one would you be and why?" Or, "How many manholes are in New York City?"

I think these types of questions are ridiculous. Google famously asked questions like this in the past, but has now ended that practice. The problem is they do not truly assess the candidate's ability to perform the role. Some may say they demonstrate critical-thinking skills, but I believe you should assess that using real, role-specific scenarios. As a result, I would not worry about these types of questions being asked. If you do get asked them, your answer on the spot will likely be fine—just explain your thought process. You will not be rejected from a position because your favorite animal is the extinct saber-toothed tiger.

What if I am wrong with the 10 traits I selected?

You may never know exactly which traits a company is looking for. Getting the traits 100% correct is not the point of Action 1. The traits help you to identify relevant example stories. The example stories in turn help you demonstrate your value in ways that are most likely relevant to that position. Do not fret over the traits too much.

Do you have any tips for phone interviews?

All of the preparation methods mentioned thus far apply to any type of interview, whether it's in person or over the phone. Phone interviews can be difficult for some people, since you cannot get a good read on facial cues, body language, etc. To make the best impression on a phone interview, I recommend the following:

1. Dress up.
   This may sound strange, but I tell the folks I assist to dress as if they were doing the interview in person. This keeps your brain focused a bit more versus doing an interview in your sweatpants, which may put your mind in a more relaxed state. There is no science behind this recommendation, just anecdotal evidence I have observed in my own interviews and from others' feedback.

2. Sit up.
   The sound of your voice can be used to help make a positive first impression on phone interviews. Therefore, I recommend paying attention to your posture while on the phone. If you slouch, the tone of your voice may change. Try it out and see for yourself. The human ear can detect the subtle changes in tone. You want to sound attentive, energized, and alert. Sit up!

3. Take notes.
   Have a notebook and writing implement ready to take notes. I encourage this for in-person interviews as well. Your interviewer will be jotting down notes about you, so why not do the same as you learn new things about the role? You also can have some questions

handy, and write down additional questions you may think of as the interview progresses. The notebook also comes in handy when you have a lot of interviewers—write their names down so you do not forget who is who.

4. Smile.
    When someone smiles while they speak to you over the phone you can hear it in their voice. A smile makes the slightest change in tone, and exudes positivity. I am not suggesting forcing a smile or holding a smile the entire interview. I am just pointing it out because it can add a bit of warmth to your voice when appropriate.

The above also applies to videoconference interviews. In addition, you will want to make sure whatever is visible through your web cam is tidy and professional.

Speaking of smiling, what if my interviewers do not smile or are stone-faced the entire time?

I am unsure why in some organizations people make interviews seem like poker matches. Ultimately, the interviewers may be trying to protect themselves (think HR issues) by not giving away too many clues as to whether they want to hire you or not. This seems a bit unnatural to me.

If this does happen to you, I suggest sticking to your plan and continuing to be yourself. If you like to smile, then do not stop smiling just because they are not reciprocating.

What do I wear to an interview?

I like to ask what the attire of the office is before I go in for an interview. Then, I will wear just slightly over what is deemed to be standard dress. When it doubt, overdress.

What if they ask me for a weakness?

Many people wonder if they should provide weaknesses if asked to do so. I do not see any problem with this, as long as you state what you are doing to improve those weaknesses.

Weaknesses do not have to be things you have never completed or tried to do before. Rather, they can be areas that you think you need to improve. Self-awareness and continuous learning are positive traits, so end your responses to weakness questions with those.

Take Joe as an example, who just recently was promoted to management. He knew he needed to improve on giving critical feedback to the people he managed. Joe had delivered tough feedback to others before, but felt he could be better at conveying the message. During his interview, Joe stated that as a weakness, but followed up with the fact that he currently is listening to an audiobook about providing feedback, and has seen improvement already in what he applied thus far.

When do I talk about compensation?

I always recommend waiting until the offer is formalized before discussing salary.

Sometimes, however, HR or recruiters may demand to know what you expect before setting up an interview. In this case, you need to do your homework in order to understand the market rates really well and be prepared with facts.

It is best to try to obtain the salary range of the job you are applying for first. If you are asked for your salary expectations, you can try to ask something like, "What is the typical range paid to employees at this level in your company?" If it is above what you are expecting, great! If not, then you can give your range of what you were looking for, and ask what can be done to help minimize the gap. Remember, there are other important aspects of compensation than just salary. Benefits like a sign-on bonus, additional vacation days, 401(k) matching, relocation bonus, healthcare plans, work from home days, and so on, can help to bridge a salary gap. Assess what works best for you and your situation.

Notice above I said the word salary *range*. I do not suggest giving a single number for your salary expectations. Doing that makes it sound like you will only settle on that one number and nothing else. Employers want to hire folks who are flexible and will work together to find a solution. Getting to an agreeable compensation structure in a fair and levelheaded manner is good for both parties. Think of it as the beginning of a great relationship; you want to get started on the right foot.

Of course, if you are in a position where you can walk away (especially in the case where you have a higher offer from another company), then you have the upper hand. Use it to your advantage, but do not go overboard. Make it clear you want to work there, but that you have another offer at a higher salary. Be honest, but open to making things work.

Do I need to have questions ready to ask of my interviewers?

Most definitely.

When candidates fail to ask me any questions at all, I take it to mean they are not really interested.

I encourage all candidates to use questions as a way to gauge if the company is a right fit. In other words, the interview is not a one-way street; it is an opportunity for you to assess them as well. Will you like working there? Does the company culture jibe with your expectations? Is the role what you really want to be doing?

Here are some questions to consider asking:
- What type of career trajectory does this role have?

- What have others in this role gone on to do?
- What are the things you like the best about working here?
- What is the company culture like?
- How will my performance be evaluated?
- What are some of the challenges someone may face in this role?
- How does the company incorporate new ideas?
- What is more important to you: customer happiness or employee happiness?

Some of the most impactful questions I received from candidates during interviews did not appear to be rehearsed. These are questions they thought of mid-interview based on things I said or described about the role. That shows active listening—a great trait for any role.

Should I send a thank you note to my interviewers?

Yes. Thank you notes are good form. The goal is to reaffirm your interest in the role, and thank them for taking the time to meet with you. Thank you notes also help to keep you top of mind. Try to send your note within 24 hours of the interview. If you met with multiple individuals, send a note to each person.

These days, an email thank you note is just fine. However, use your judgment based on the type of role or industry. For example, if you are applying for a position at a printing company, you may want to send a printed note on nice quality paper in the mail.

Thank you notes, like everything else I have mentioned in this book, should be brief and to the point. They can follow a similar three-step structure as well:

- *Intro.* Thank them for meeting with you and giving details about the role and company.
- *Middle.* Reaffirm your interest based on what you learned about the role and how it matches the specific skill sets you have.
- *End.* Express your excitement in hearing back from them.

A good thank you note will never look generic. Try to personalize it based on things you spoke about. This will demonstrate your attention to detail and thoughtfulness.

Conclusion

Thank you for reading my book. I hope it inspires the confidence you need to get that new job. If so, get in touch at StephenASurace.com and let me know how it went. I look forward to hearing from you.